CONTENTS

EVERYTHING

IS WELCOME

Sometimes you may wonder, with all the work you've done on yourself over the years, with all the self-help books you've read and all the spiritual classes and therapy sessions you've attended, why the present moment still feels so . . . *incomplete? Unfinished? Unresolved?*

Why, after all these years, does your heart still feel tender and broken and raw? Why won't your mind stop spinning and churning, even though you've tried to quiet it down with every kind of technique from every well-meaning spiritual guru, therapist, or life coach? Why do you still feel far from where you hoped you would be by now?

Sometimes the present moment just feels so *unwelcomable*, doesn't it? So hot, uncomfortable, restless, boring, or painful that we long to be *anywhere other than here*. Sometimes acceptance, love, peace, surrender, joy, bliss, high vibes, healing, and spiritual awakening seem like a happy dream . . . meant for other people.

Sometimes it just feels like you must be fundamentally broken or damaged in some way.

I want you to hear and keep hearing the simple teaching that saved my life. *There is nothing wrong with you.* You are exactly where you should be right now, having the experience you are meant to be having, feeling the pain or discomfort or longing or numbness or *incompleteness* you are supposed to be feeling, or not feeling, in this precise instant of your life.

This present moment can never truly go wrong, just like the weather can never truly go wrong. We may not like the rain or the fog, but eventually we have to accept that it is happening, and is not some cosmic error or punishment from a vengeful or sadistic god. It is our *resistance* to the present moment, our often unconscious attempts to push away thoughts and feelings and desires, to run from them, abandon them, even destroy them within ourselves, that creates so much of our depression, stress, anxiety and fear, and ultimately exhaustion and spiritual and psychological burnout. Refusing to be here, in the moment we're in, right in the moment we're in it, is disempowering, fatiguing, and ultimately an exercise in futility, like cursing at the fog, or yelling at the raindrops as they fall.

How can we *welcome* the present moment, then? How does this surrender to "what is" happen? Is it something we can do, or something that transpires by grace? Is it possible to welcome the unwelcomable parts of ourselves, the boredom, the discomfort, the inner heat and ice and fog, the nonacceptance itself?

This is what I have learned: Even our depression, fear, and exhaustion contain supreme intelligence and healing power. There is simply no part of us that is wrong or bad, inhuman or inherently dishonorable. There is no part of us that is "unspiritual" or sinful and unworthy of love. Your sadness, your fear, your urges, your doubts, your deepest feelings of loneliness and despair—even your longing to die, if it comes—are not mistakes, not sick or bad or wrong, not signs of your failure or your lack of spiritual or psychological evolution. *They are vital parts of you, revered visitors of the present moment, just longing to be touched with love and understanding and breath.* Your "wounds" are not aberrations or faults in your system, or signs that you are beyond repair or "too sensitive" for this world; they are the lead, the base metal, the undigested elements of your psyche waiting to be alchemically transmuted into gold. There is simply no part of you that does not belong, no weather that is fundamentally unwelcome in the sky of your awareness.

The poems in this book emerged from a very deep place inside of me over a period of several years. Many of them I don't actually remember writing; I only remember watching, astonished, as they formed themselves on the page. They are here to remind you that you are never completely alone, that no matter how dark it seems, how lost you feel, or how far off the path you think you've strayed, healing is always possible, and that no thought or feeling or desire or ache is an aberration. And that even when you feel you cannot bear another moment, something bigger is already bearing you, holding you, supporting you. Something vast and mysterious is giving you life, willing you on, even when you have lost the personal will to go on. The same divine brilliance that was there at the Big Bang, the same unspeakable life force that grows the grass and makes the sun shine and animates all living things, the same inspiration that created this book and wrote these words and reads them now, is breathing you, beating your heart, moment by moment, pumping hot blood around your body, giving you the courage and strength to hold as much as you are holding, feel as much as you are feeling, know as much as you can possibly know from where you are.

I speak as one who has known suffering, trauma, unbearable shame, anxiety, and fear. Life forced me to travel to the traumatic depths of myself, to face and take care of my deepest pain and self-loathing and infuse it with loving awareness, to give my "inner child" what it was asking for. Attention. Breath. *Myself.*

Once I wanted to die, and now I want to live.

Each of these poems is a *meditation*, designed to soothe, encourage, or lovingly provoke you, to invite you out of your mind and back into your body, to arouse your deepest authentic truth, help you feel your deepest feelings, and help you navigate back to your true home: *the present moment*. Take time to digest these poems. You might put the book down between readings, breathe deeply, and contemplate what you've just read. If something I say upsets you, annoys you, makes you feel really uncomfortable, triggers an old pain, a fear, a sorrow, or even a new joy or powerful urge toward *more life*, *trust* that this part of you just wants to be met today. Slow down. Get really curious about your somatic or emotional visitor. Drench it with awareness. Invite it to sit with you, walk with you, cry with you, swim with you, scream with you, dance with you, meditate with you. If you find yourself really struggling, talk to a safe friend, or a healer or therapist. Or sit under the sky and commune with the clouds, the stars, the gods, the moon, the mountains, the oceans, the Earth. Ask your inner child what he or she needs today. For she may hold all the answers, or at least all the courage to find them.

Sometimes you have to break a little more to heal a little more. Healing is truly paradoxical, and the path of awakening only leads us back *here* in the end. Stop trying to work it all out and just let yourself be exactly as you are today. No matter what's happened to you in the past, no matter what you are going through in your life in the present, no matter what your future holds, you can always *begin again* where you are. Here. Right here . . .

With a simple breath. With an ache or a loneliness. With a relaxed body or a tense body. With a sinking feeling in the belly or a rush of excitement in the chest. With an open heart or a closed one, with a despair or an inexplicable joy. With a clenched jaw, a pressure between the eyes, a tension in the back or shoulders. With the sound of a dog barking or the easy laughter of a child. With a cup of tea with a dear friend. With your own refusal or unwillingness to begin. With your own courage, or utter lack of courage. With whatever picture life is painting for you, right now, on the brilliant canvas of your present-moment awareness.

I hope you enjoy these poems, little loving transmissions direct from my heart to yours.

PART ONE

A FIELD OF MEDITATION

Here's what meditation really is: touching life exactly where life is touching you.

When we meditate, we aren't trying to change or manipulate our experience. We aren't trying to access some higher or transcendent state, zone out of our humanity, or become some spiritually enlightened guru. We aren't trying to silence the mind, destroy the ego, free ourselves from difficult feelings, or even "feel better." We aren't even trying to relax, calm down, or be at peace, however odd that sounds to the goal- and future-focused mind.

Simply begin by embracing the part of you that doesn't want to embrace, be embraced, or even begin. You can always begin there. I have begun thousands of meditations with the part of me that doesn't want to meditate. It is such an old friend. I love it dearly.

So, begin. Now. Simply feel your feet on the ground. Notice the mysterious alive sensations there, without trying to alter or understand them. Notice the location of your hands right now as they hold this book, their position, their weight, the way the fingers are curling, their heat, their aliveness. What does it feel like to hold a book? Imagine it was your first time ever holding a book. Notice the way your face feels as you read this. Does your face feel tense or relaxed? Is your forehead creased? Your jaw slightly tense? What is the expression on your face as you read these words? Is there a smile or a frown on your lips? Is there a pressure or contraction in your shoulders? Notice the weight and density of your body. How it gently sinks into the chair or sofa you're sitting on. How it feels to wear the clothes you are wearing, where they touch your shoulders, your hips, your legs, their bulk and weight and texture. What it feels like to be alive, right now. What it feels like to be . . . *you*. Uniquely, unrepeatably you, having the experience you're having, on this very ordinary day of your life. This day has never come before, and it will never come again. Will you greet it with your curiosity? Will you bless it with your attention?

Even if you notice a sense of struggle in yourself, there's no need to *struggle against the struggle* either. Struggling against struggle only creates more struggle. Instead, bless even the struggle, allow even the struggle, for it too is life, and deserves to be here in our meditation together.

Instead of going to war with this moment and trying to push it away or make it better, more comfortable, more exciting, more spiritual, or more whole, can you open your heart and your awareness and *receive* it as it is, discomfort and mess and stickiness and all? True meditation just means *being awake and alive to this precious moment*. It means attention without a goal. This is the kind of meditation the Buddha taught.

Consider that you are exactly where you need to be right now. Anxious, depressed, empty, happy, fed up, frustrated, lost, numb, spaced-out, angry, or just feeling far from life . . . Paradoxically, you are exactly where you are supposed to be, supported and held by forces mysterious and ancient and unnameable.

AND

YOU

NEED

NO

PROOF

Slow down. Take the day one breath at a time.
You stand on sacred ground, always.

For it is your last day.
And your first day.

You are dying, today. So live!

Get curious. Allow yourself to not know what's coming
in the *next* moment.
Invite attention into *this* unique moment.

What is it like, to be here?
To see?
To taste?
To smell?
To feel? To not feel?

To be alive,
on this day of all days?

Laugh at the voices in your head.
(They are not who you really are.)

You are powerful.
You are worthy.

You belong.

And you need no proof,

THE
SHADOWS
AND
THE
LIGHT

Wanting to live,
and wanting to die.

Wanting to break into newness,
and wanting to hide.

Wanting to connect,
and wanting to be alone.

Wanting to want,
and wanting to be free from want.

Child, you hold *all* of this sacredness
in your vast and beautiful heart.

Never turn away from any part, my love.
Yet never let any part be your master.

Live right in the middle.
Be free and wild in the middle
like the trees in the forest:

Reach out for the light, yes,
but love your shadows too.

THE

COURAGE

TO

STOP

RUNNING

Trauma is the invisible force
that keeps us running, restless,
in pursuit of some intangible goal.

Caught up in some unnecessary activity.
Addiction. Compulsions. Distractions.
Makes us escape into thinking.
Makes the body feel unsafe.
Makes the present moment into an enemy.

If we slow down.

If we stop.

If we rest.

If we simply do nothing.

Then we will have to face . . . ourselves.

We will have to face buried feelings.

All the shit we were running from.

All the darkness.

The gunk.

The muck.

The loneliness.

The aches and the boredom.

The night and the emptiness.

Trauma says, "Run!"

Trauma says, "Do Not Stop!"

Trauma says, "Just keep going!"

Trauma says, "Stopping is unsafe!"

We start by proving to ourselves
that it is safe to rest! Safe to be still.
Safe to do nothing, just for a moment.
Safe to think our thoughts and feel our feelings . . .

. . . and not "fix" the moment in any way.

We can begin—one moment at a time—
to digest all the undigested things inside.
Stay with sadness for a moment longer.
Be present with our joy or shame for an instant more.
Breathe into our anxiety instead of running from it.

Become curious about our discomfort
instead of distracting ourselves with unnecessary food,
drink,
cleaning,
drugs,
sex,
shopping,
Internet,
thinking,
talking,
overworking,
yoga,
seeking,
more thinking,
rumination,
fantasy and false hope.

We can challenge the core story at the heart of trauma:
That the *present moment is unsafe*.
That the body is somehow working *against* us.
That feelings, sensations, or thoughts are *dangerous*.
That stillness and silence equal nonexistence and
death.

And that we have to "do" something
in order to be worthy,
and loved,
and whole.

It takes courage to stop running.
It takes courage to lean into the storm.
It takes courage to touch the darkness inside
with the infinite light of our curious attention.

It takes courage to break the addiction to *futures*.

And be present.

And breathe.

And *not know*.

LET
LOVE
GO

Forget about "transcending" the body.
Love it instead.

Let go of the idea of "letting go."
Instead, *let love go* deep into the tender places,
the parts that ache.

Inhale into your sadness.
Let your fear move deep within you.
Bow to your uncertainty.

There is an untouchable place in you
that fearlessly allows itself to be touched.

Here, even your unworthiness has worth.
And that old feeling that you are unlovable?
It is loveable here.

Presence is the container, never the contained.
There is so much room in you, friend. So much room.
The Unknown embraces all that is known.

In the certainty of yourself,
even uncertainty can be held like a newborn.

There is nothing wrong with you,
including the idea
that there is something wrong with you.

So stop trying to love yourself;
simply be the Self that loves.

BETWEEN

THE

LINES

I want you to pay attention
   to the   spaces,
the silences, the pauses, the   gaps between
         the words,
the white   of the page behind the black
         of the ink,
the calm   that holds the chaos   that spins through
this ever-turning world and I want to remind you

of the beauty of the unspoken,
the sweetness of the unresolved,

the invisible screen that holds the light and the shade
and the mystery that permeates everything,

the mystery that wrote these words
(and the very same mystery that is reading them now)

and is paying attention to the   spaces,
the   gaps, the pauses,   the endings that begin
new conversations, and the stillness
that envelops
us
all

LISTEN

FROM

SILENCE

Be present. Be here.
The teaching is so ridiculously simple.
Be present. Be here.

Feel your feet on the ground, your belly rising and falling.
Be open and receptive to the life all around you.

The sounds, smells, tastes. Feelings rising unexpectedly.
A tingling in the belly. A contraction in the throat.
Heaviness in the head. An old melancholy coming to visit.
Stay curious as the moment dances.
Stay curious even as you lose your curiosity.

Listen. Listen with your entire body.
Hear yourself. Hear the person you're talking to.
Hear the silence in between the sentences.
Let the silence linger a little while longer.
Move just a little into the discomfort.

There's no rush. There's no "better" moment to get to.
Silence doesn't always need to be filled.

Be a little more naked. A little slower.
Know a little less what you're about to say.
Be a little less prepared, a little messier,
a little more willing to expose your shaky, vulnerable heart.

Be surprised at your own responses.
Don't numb yourself with the same old stories.
Stumble if you need to. It's okay. You are held.

Let your words emerge from silence and return
to them.

Notice if you're talking just to avoid the silence.
Notice if you're regurgitating a story you've told before.
Notice if you're trying to impress, or win love.
Or avoid being seen for who you really are.

Friend, in silence we can truly meet.
Genuine understanding is beyond mind.

Let us be awkward and shy and hesitant together.
And clumsy. I don't mind.

Love is wordless; she needs no more words.
Listen to the silence; it is volcanic.

Be present. Be here.
The teaching is so damn simple.
Be present. Be here.

THIS
IS
MEDITATION

Let what comes, come. Let what goes, go.

Don't try to push away what comes.

(It's already here and it will pass by itself in time.)

Don't try to cling to what goes.

(Grief is natural. Leaving is life. Bless the leaving too.)

Let what stays, stay.

Let what dies, die.

Let what lives, live.

Stop interfering with *the way of things* today.

Just be the wide open space for all of it.
Every thought, every feeling.
Every moment of boredom or doubt.

Be the awareness. Be the ocean.
Allow these waves.

This is meditation, your authentic Self.

THE
SACRED
LOTUS

Oh, our innocent, tender hearts!
Our tender, innocent hearts!

We open, we close.
We close, we open,
like the Sacred Lotus in the warmth of the sun,
like the ocean's tides going in and out.

The goal is not to "stay open" all the time,
to shame the closing,
to attack ourselves
when we are "less than" what we could be.

There is no goal except the looking, the seeing itself,
the willingness to turn toward our experience,
come out of the narrative of time and turn toward the
present tenderness,
drench our aching hearts with attention,
saturate our closed hearts with understanding,
illuminate the painful moment
in the brilliant light of awareness.

Not to fix, not to fix, but to come closer.

Not to transform. But to transmit,
to transmit all our love,
all of our kindness
into what's here,
like a mother holding her newborn,
like a lover holding her beloved,
like God
holding her creation with such reverence.

Like God in awe of her creation, yes.
Hold yourself like this.
In every Now.

Oh, our innocent, tender hearts!
Our tender, innocent hearts!

We open, we close.
We close, we open.

Like the ocean's tides going in and out,
like the Sacred Lotus
in the warmth of the sun.

INTO

THE

BELLY

OF

MEDITATION

You are weary, friend.
Sit.
You are thirsty.
Here. Drink.

You are hungry. Here. Take this.
A piece of bread.
A small bowl of soup.
See how God has taken form!
It is all I have but it will keep you alive.

I will light a fire that will never go out.
A sacred flame. Unconditional in its burning.
To illuminate us in the darkness.

Oh. I see you are wounded.
Bruised. Bleeding.
Exhausted from the world.
You have suffered much, I know.

Come.

Take off these dirty rags.

Don't worry. It's safe.

There is strength in your nakedness.

Here. Wash.

Rub this medicine onto your wounds.

Put on these robes, they are clean and dry.

Lie down. Close your eyes.

I will watch over us tonight.

Listen. You have not failed.
I see new life breaking through.
I see birth. An insurrection.
The sharp edge of hope.

I have no teaching for you.
No wise words.

I only want you to trust what you are going through.
To bring this fire inside of you.
Until the end.

I have known this pain. *Yes.*
This courage to keep moving. *Yes.*
This courage to rest, too.
The sacrifice of the known world.

Friend.

Drop into the belly of meditation now.

The place you were always seeking.

The vast silence at the Earth's core which is your own core.

Breathing into the gut now.

The throat. The chest.

Irradiating the nervous system with unspeakable tenderness.

Flooding the body with soft, warm light.

Drenching the human form with divine love.

And sleep.

And sleep.

I may not be here when you wake.
We may not meet again in form.

Yet I leave you with all you need.
Food. Water. A bed.
A chance to rest.
A touch of kindness.

And your unbreakable Self.

PART TWO

SAYING YES TO THE MESS

t is exhausting trying to be good, kind, loving, selfless, fault-less, perfect, the best, highly evolved, the most spiritual. It is such a relief when you start to allow yourself to be imperfect and human again, when you begin to *bless the mess* of your vulnerable, ever-changing, and unpredictable mortal self.

Trauma is simply "stuck life energy," spontaneous feelings, desires, and impulses that were not allowed to flow when they first emerged in the body. Perhaps it wasn't safe to let powerful thoughts and feelings, impulses and desires move in you back then, and you weren't taught how to experience them or express them safely. You didn't know how to let them emerge in you, honor them, love them, and let them move on. And so these energies—terror, rage, loneliness, despair, excitement, joy, desire—got stuck and frozen in your body, starved of warmth, starved of oxygen, starved of light and trust and attention. It's not your fault, dear one. You were only trying to be loved and protect yourself from harm.

Oh, the truth you wanted to speak! The words you wanted to scream. The tears you longed to cry. The uncontrolled, wild ways in which you wanted to move your body. The healthy human responses, the urges, and yearnings you intelligently squished down in order to win love, stay safe, even stay alive.

The authenticity your body needed to express, but couldn't.

The good news is that today is a new day. Anything stuck in you yesterday can be given permission to move again today, in the safety of the present moment. The Now is the *only* place where life can emerge, be digested, and healed (returned to the whole). This will take courage, the willingness to feel old pain and breathe through it, and trust the body today instead of giving in to the mind and its age-old fears.

In the safety of your own presence, or in the safe presence of another being (imagined or real) who can hold you and trust your process, can you turn toward the sore place, the tight place, the dark place, the aching place, the frightened place, the anxious place, and bring to it the light of your awareness, the light of love? For it is love that truly heals. A love that welcomes all.

Life only wants to play in you, to dance, vibrate, shake, flutter, and surge through to completion. The impulses and urges, the desires and callings you learned were "sick" or "dangerous" or "wrong" or "shameful" were *always* natural, and normal, and healthy, and infused with infinite intelligence. They won't damage or break you as you turn toward them now and give them the love and attention and the safe passage they always deserved. You don't have to "give in" to them or obey them. You don't have to act them out. Just *feel* them, shine the light of loving awareness on them. Bow to them as if you were bowing to something infinitely precious and sacred within.

Be a vast Heart now, a loving curious welcoming Heart. Trust this intelligent dark storm of feeling as it emerges, roars, and passes in its own time. Your wounds, your turbulent and sorrowful places, your imperfections, are not mistakes; they are *the places in you desperately yearning for love*, waiting to be penetrated with a curious Light.

So scream, shake, tremble, weep, sweat, doubt your sanity, make a holy mess—you are a warrior and you are alive and you are healing and learning to *play* again. Through the pain, to the glory!

BOW

TO

EVERYTHING

Bow to confusion!
It is the fertile ground
from which great clarity blossoms
in its own sweet time.

It is not confusing, when you bow.

Bow to anger! It contains the power
of life itself. It roars universes into form.
It rises suddenly to protect the organism.
It values your unique voice.
It gives you courage to speak up.

There is no violence, when you bow.

Bow to sorrow. It keeps the heart soft.
It grounds you in an awareness
of impermanence and change and loss.
It brings compassion for all beings who weep and
seek a new home.

It is not depressing, when you bow.

Bow to fear.

She is only trying to protect you

from what you are not yet ready or willing to face.

She guides you gently into the Unknown.

You are not afraid,
when you bow.

LET

A

FEELING

CRACK

YOU

OPEN

Here's the bad news:

You can't get "over" a feeling.
You can't get "past" it.
You can't release it.
You can't let go of it.
You can't transform or transmute it.
You can't even heal it.

These ideas all come from the mind,
not awareness itself.

They are all subtle forms of violence,
sneaky ways of saying no to a feeling,
hoping for its disappearance, its death.

We learn to let go of "letting go."
We release the very idea of "release."
We heal from our exhausting efforts to "heal."

We offer, instead, our simple presence.
Our nonresistant attention.
Our love.

Here's the good news:

In this field of presence
the feeling is no longer a problem, an enemy,
an aberration, a stain, a block to freedom or peace.
It is no longer "something wrong."
It is no longer "negative."
It is no longer unsafe, a threat.

It is no longer an unwanted, unloved, neglected child.
You are now its guardian, its protector, its loving
parent,
its Home.

And held lightly, in a still space of allowing,
the feeling stays for a while, or moves on,
or returns, or never returns,
but either way, you are healed
from the need to find healing elsewhere.

You do not heal feelings, you see,
they heal you, when you allow them
to guide you back to your original Wholeness,
your loving nature,
your breath,
your rightful place on this Earth.

ON

COURAGE

Courage is your willingness to *not know*.

> To speak your truth.
> To walk your path.
> To face ridicule and rejection.
> To keep going, despite the voices in your
> head
> and the judgments of others.

And there are no guarantees you will *make it*
to the place you thought you were headed.

But you will *make it* to a destination even more glorious:
Yourself.

Nobody can walk for you!
You walk in radical aloneness,
naked in the face of life, no protection, no crutches,
no external authority.
No ideology to save you.

    No promises anymore.
    Only the beating of the heart,
    and the air in the lungs, and the thrill and terror
    of being utterly free,
    no longer numb to yourself.

And a knowing from deep within.
And the call of your ancestors.

    And the ground holding you.
    And the sun warming your tired body.

And the fragrance of love everywhere.
And warm tears running down your cheeks.

    And this gorgeous vulnerability
    that has made you completely indestructible.

VICTORY!

You don't have to be the best.
You don't have to win.
You only have to be *yourself*.

You only have to be real.

And speak from the heart.

And know that you have the right to see how you see,

and think how you think, and feel what you feel,

and desire what you desire.

You don't have to be a success in the eyes of the world

and you don't have to be an expert on living.

You only have to offer what you offer,
breathe how you breathe, make mistakes and screw
up
and learn to love your stumbling and say the
wrong thing
and stop worrying so much about impressing anyone
because in the end you only have to live with yourself
and joy is not given but found in the deepest
recesses of your being
so there can be joy in falling and joy in making
mistakes
and joy in making a fool of yourself and joy in
forgetting joy
and then holding yourself close as you crumble to
the ground
and weep out the old dreams.

Joy is closeness
with the one you love:
You.

You don't have to be the best.
You really don't have to win.

You only have to remember this intimacy with
the sky, the nearness of the mountains and feel the sun
warming your shoulders and the nape of your neck

and know that you are alive,
and that you are a *success* at being alive,
and that you have won already,
and you are victorious already,
without having to prove
a damn
thing.

To *anyone*.

YOU

ARE

FREE

Live.
Make mistakes.
Screw everything up.
But live anyway.

Taste failure. Taste success.

See how in the end, they taste the same.

They taste of *you*. They taste of *life*.

They taste of the love you always sought.

So live.

Make mistakes.

Screw everything up.

Say the right thing.

Say the wrong thing.

Shake, sweat, let the heart race and pound.

Find your edge and never abandon it.

They will call you names.

An idiot. Afraid.

Deluded. Mad. Not quite yourself anymore.

Yes!

So taste rejection. Taste disapproval.

Taste the absence of any taste.

But hold yourself close. Breathe.

And live. Love.

Yes.

Break open to love.

Make mistakes.

Screw everything up.

Fall to the ground, laughing, crying,

celebrating the fall.

The ground will hold you.

And you are free.

DO

IT

REAL

Today.
Lose a few friends.
Offend a few people.
Say *no* if you mean no.
Say *yes* if you mean yes.

> Nice little boys and girls
> never win mommy or daddy's love anyway.
> They only become beggars.

Stop trying to do it right.
Do it real instead.

You don't have to win love.
Only live it.

> Weep. Wail. Laugh like you did
> when you were young and
> didn't care what people thought.

Speak your uncomfortable truth without apology.
Let your heart break.
Let your certainties crumble.

Be a blubbering mess on the ground of love.

Life is too short to hold it all together.
You have longed to fall apart.

You will lose "safety"
but you will feel
so alive.

SHIT

WARRIORS

Sometimes,
despite your best intentions and efforts,
despite your incredible "spiritual progress,"
you just feel like . . . shit.

So, feel like shit today!

Where is the problem
when you dive fearlessly into the heart
of *that* unique experience?

Feel like shit, but consciously so!
Flush that wound with curiosity!
Dive in, knowingly!

"Feeling like shit"
can be the most spiritual feeling of all,
a unique gateway to grace,
as sacred as the most profound joy,
as holy as the most transcendent, ecstatic bliss.

You forge a new spirituality
in each moment you stay in that broken place,
infusing the shitty sadness with your brilliant light,
permeating the shitty loneliness with attention.

This could save the world:
brothers and sisters courageous enough
to feel like shit,
without numbing themselves
or turning away from their shitty pain.

Warriors of shit.

Shit warriors.

Let's start a revolution.

WHEN YOUR PATH IS YOUR FEET

Take the step.

Shiver, tremble, shake, vomit, wet yourself.
Feel more fear than you've ever felt!

But take the step.

Or do not. (That's okay too.)

Either way, stand where you stand today.
This is all you need to know:
Stand where you stand today.

Feel your feet in contact with this sacred ground.
Your presence sanctifies it.

Let doubts surge. Let terrors surge.
Let all the shaming and fearful voices surge.

Bless all the surging ones.
They cannot break you now
or knock you off your path.

     Nothing can knock you off your path.
     When your path *is* your feet.
     When your heart *is* the road.

When you breathe in horizons.

TRUST
THE
PAIN

Friend, the ache you feel today
is not a mistake. There is no shame
in what you are going through.

In some distant world
you are being hailed as a warrior-hero.

Your pain is a holy site, an altar.

Come out of the mind and into the body now.

Send attention deep into the raw sensations

in your belly, chest, throat, head.

Dress today's wounds with presence.

Breathe into the sadness.

Offer the anger oxygen.

Infuse the fearful one with fearless fascination.

Don't try to "fix" the burning.
(It's not yours to fix, it belongs to the ages.)

Don't try to "get rid" of it.
(The heart does not understand "get rid of.")

Don't even try to "transmute" it.
That is not your job.
Your only job is to *love* what's here.

And to love your own inability to love
and to have courage, or to have no courage today,
to be as present as you can possibly be,
and not an ounce more.

You are giving birth to new life,
to a precious inner child,
love and pain making something new,
wound as womb.

She is scared, she is raw, she is a little heartbroken,
but she is so alive now, and deserving of love.

The *ache* in you is the place
where alchemy longs to happen.

PART THREE

THE COURAGE
TO STAND ALONE

I t can be scary when we are called to confront our aloneness, the seemingly infinite depths of that empty, homeless feeling inside of us. When all our old protections fall away and the abandoned and neglected ones inside come begging for our love and attention.

It can feel sometimes as though there's nowhere to turn, like we want to crawl out of our own skin, urgently get out of the Now and into some other time or place. We may dream of easy escape, some way to numb the pain of the gaping hole in our hearts. Some of us may even dream of suicide. I know I did, for many, many years.

It takes bravery to stop, breathe, and—slowly, slowly, slowly—turn back toward the lonely, dark, empty "void" inside (in reality, there is no void). To actually turn to face the sense of abandonment buried deep within our guts, to soften into the sense of separation that has been with us for as long as we can remember. We don't have to make the feeling go away today, only lean into it, breathe into it, begin to make room for it, maybe even learn to trust its presence.

As I write this, a memory floats onto the screen of my awareness: entering my dear father's bedroom some months before he died, finding him gently sobbing to himself. I'd never seen my dad cry before, or show any vulnerability lest he be seen as weak or crazy. He noticed me and beckoned me to come closer.

"What's the matter, Dad?"

He told me, *"Son, I am so scared of being alone."*

My heart instantly opened at such a vulnerable, unprotected, undefended admission from a man who had always been so emotionally closed and untouchable. In these sacred moments at the end of his life, raw truth was emerging. Shamed and repressed heartache was coming up to be felt, loved, blessed before he passed on. In that lonely bedroom a strange paradox revealed itself: We had never felt so connected to each other. Profoundly alone, we embraced each other in the midst of our aloneness, and the Gates of Heaven parted, if only for a minute.

"We are here together, now, Dad."

Perhaps loneliness is like a cosmic nostalgia, a preverbal memory of a deep womb-connection, with ourselves, with the planet, with every being who has ever lived. In leaning into our own loneliness, shame, and existential anxiety, we may be able to touch into compassion for the loneliness of every human being, for every heart longing to connect, for every grieving heart, every frightened heart.

We are alone, yet never alone. This is the great paradox of existence. Our loneliness, when not resisted or numbed away, may actually end up connecting us more deeply to life and each other, like it did for me and my sweet father that winter evening.

Let us learn to be alone, then! Alone, without distraction, which is true meditation. Alone, communing with the breath as it rises and falls. Alone with the mind and its incredible dance. Alone with the rain and the morning sun. Alone with the crackle of autumn leaves under our feet, or the crunch of winter snow. Alone with the hopes and joys and anxieties of this human form, living a single day on this remarkable planet. Alone with our precious selves, with this unfathomable sense of connection to all things, with birth and loss and death and their myriad mysteries.

Alone, with all of life.

A

RECOGNITION

I don't know you,
and you don't know me;
we discover each other
in the Unknown.

It is possible
that we met five billion years ago
at the formation of a star
and have been drawn back to each other
by some kind of divine loneliness,
God's mad yearning
for herself.

Loneliness is not a negative thing,
it is the *gravity of love*,
a brilliantly intelligent nostalgia
that pulls lovers back to each other,
keeps them on the path
and prevents them from settling for less
than the kind of love that endures
five billion years of burning.

Forgetting, remembering, forgetting,
like breathing, like the tides going in and out.

    I don't know you,
    and you don't know me,
    but we recognize each other,
    here in the Vastness.

FORGET

UNCONDITIONAL

LOVE

Forget unconditional love. Forget loving perfectly.
Forget having a permanently open heart.
You can't do it.
It's an impossible goal that, paradoxically,
makes you violent inside.

Your inner child rebels against *any* spiritual ideal.

You cannot *do* unconditional love.

But you can embrace your imperfect attempts to love,

your failure to reach the goals,

your disappointment,

your exquisite shame,

your ecstasy and your agony too.

You can bless your inherited conditional ideas of love.

You can celebrate your messy, deeply human,

totally conditioned attempts to love,

in unconditional present awareness.

Friend, even your failure to love unconditionally
is welcome here,

unconditionally.

That is the true meaning of unconditional love:
the love that smiles at our *trying* too.

THE
SECRET
OF
ALL
HEALING

Don't try to love yourself.

The "trying" is the self-hatred.

The "trying" is exactly what depletes you.

Instead, make room for the part that doesn't love.

Or doesn't know how.

Or mistrusts love. Or was never taught it.

Hold that fragile part of you in loving awareness.

Breathe into the battle inside.

Infuse your nonacceptance with inquisitive attention.

Immerse your frustration in meditation.

Don't try to love yourself.
Simply oxygenate the unloved one.

NO

PLACE

LIKE

HOME

You can *feel* abandoned, yes.
You can *feel* lonely, far from love and life,
warmth and companionship.

Others can trigger powerful feelings in you, yes.

But strip away the word,
the concept,
the story,
the thoughts you have *about* abandonment,
and return to the actuality of the living body, Now.

What does it feel like Now, this *abandonment*?
How do you know you've been *abandoned*?
Where is the evidence, in the body, today?

Attend to the sensations surging now in your belly,
chest, throat.
Feel the fluttering, pulsating, stinging sensations.
Let them grow in intensity, or dissipate, and move.
Drench the tight and tender places within
with curious, loving, agenda-free attention.
Give the sensations space; soften around them.

You've got to *breathe into yourself* now, friend,
for nobody is here to breathe into you,
and they cannot do that anyway.

The dream of love has died;
you are waking up to the reality of love.
Love does not come from without. It never did.
It was always within you. It was your power.

You only had to click your heels together.
Three times.
Click, click, click.

It was always your calling, you see,
to find a way to love yourself deeply,
to not beg for love, or seek it externally,
or wait for it, or try to hold on to it,
but to *drench yourself with it*, moment by precious moment.

Do not abandon yourself when you feel abandoned,
for there is a pain worse than abandonment:
The *abandonment of self*, the flight from where you are.
Running from yourself when you most need yourself.

Focus on "the ones who abandoned you"
and you are powerless and helpless today.
There's nothing you can do to change the past,
or others.
The present is your only place of power,
nowhere else.

Here's how to break the cycle of abandonment:
focus your love on the inner "abandoned one,"
this precious child within.

Invite loving attention deep within the belly, heart, head.
Breathe into the ground.
Feel your sorrow and your rage.
Feel your own aliveness.
Connect with these precious energies.

Ask a friend for help you if you're struggling.

Or a therapist.

Or a thousand-year-old tree.

Or a mountain.

Or the sky and all the gods and angels.

Call on the Universe for support.

Weep.

Rage.

Allow yourself to feel everything.

Cry the tears you were never allowed to cry.

Scream the screams you were never permitted to scream.

Speak the words of truth you've stifled for decades.

The *inner child is real*, and longs for you.

You have not been abandoned. Life is here.

For *you* are here.

Do you understand?

And from here, a new life grows.
As you learn to not abandon yourself,
you will, in time, attract others
who are not abandoning themselves either;
others who will not abandon you.
Who will stay with you when you cry, when you
feel lost,
and will help you stay with yourself.

When you stop abandoning yourself,
you can never be truly abandoned:
you refuse to abandon your *own* inner world,
even when others leave unexpectedly.

Nobody can abandon you: they can only move
to another place, with their own pain or joy.

Abandonment is the story of *lost love*, an old story,
for love cannot truly be lost, only rediscovered deep
within.

You are courageous enough
to be present with yourself now.
You have broken the addiction of a lifetime:
You have discovered the deep joy
of being alone.

There's no place like Home.
Click, click, click.

LONELINESS

(YOU ARE

ONE WITH

THE STARS

NOW)

Give yourself permission
to rest, and be silent,
and do nothing.

Love this aloneness, friend.
Fall into it.
(Don't worry. You won't disappear. I am here to
catch you.)

Invite warm, curious attention
deep inside your weary bones.

Until there is no loneliness,
only radical self-love.

You are full of value in this stillness.
You are richly textured in this emptiness.

There is no "original sin."
You are not *guilty* here.

Loneliness is God's gateway
to intimacy with all things.

To a great Togetherness.

You are one with the stars now.

A
PORTAL
TO
LOVE

When you're feeling sad, just feel sad.

Don't try to *not feel sad*,
you'll only split yourself in two.

Don't *think* about feeling sad.

Just feel sad.

Stay close.

Feel the raw sensations in your belly, heart, throat, head.

Let the sensations tingle, pulse, vibrate, shimmer, ache.

Give them full permission to *live*.

Breathe into them, dignify them with attention, soften around them.

(It's all just energy that wants to move in your body.)

Drop the word "sad" now.
What you feel is much bigger than a word.
Simply connect with what's here
without judging it, without moving in any direction.
Be the room for these living sensations, be their
loving embrace.
Know that these sensations aren't a mistake;
you're not doing anything wrong.

You are alive.
And sensitive.
And not numb to the body's mysteries.

You have a right to feel sad today!
To stand *with* sadness, not against it;
to be its loving parent, not its victim.
To be its protector, not its enemy.

There is no shame in sadness. No failure.
No suffering, when you can just *stay* with it.
(The suffering is always in the running away.)

Contact your sadness, and you contact the sadness of
all living beings.
Contact all living beings, and your loneliness disappears.

So just feel sad, friend;

let your sadness embrace this fragile world.

YOU

ARE

ALWAYS

HELD

When thoughts and sensations feel unbearable.
When you cannot hold yourself up.
When hope dies.
Notice, you are held.

By the Earth.

By the hills and mountains, rivers and oceans.

By the vastness of Space.

By a loving, soft Presence,

closer than breathing,

nearer than the dearest lover.

Even when you cannot bear it.
Even when you reach your limits.
Even when your strength fails
and you cannot find surrender.
The Earth has surrendered to you.

You are already held.
In the loving arms
of the Present.

Sweetheart,
even when it's unbearable,
you are already being borne.

YOU

ARE

DESTINED

FOR

LIFE

If you feel like taking your own life today, you are
not alone.
If you feel the urge to die, you are not sick or broken.

You are hurting, friend, and tired, and long for rest.
I understand. I have been there.
It is an urge as old as life itself. To die.
To shed the old skin and be made new.
To be rid of the false and touch the real.
To find deep relief from the pain of being human.
To feel the rest and finality of death.
I know this yearning well.

The urge to die is not wrong.

Many on this planet have felt the urge,

even if they will never speak of it,

even if they try to forget it, or numb it,

or distract themselves with work, food, sex, money,

easy pleasures,

or pretend to be happy and positive and "together."

You cannot distract yourself. *You* are not numb.
You feel everything so intensely.
Not everyone will understand.
(Your sensitivity is beautiful to me.)

Feel what you feel today!
Bless the part of you that longs to be somewhere else.
Let the mind scream its screams today.
You are not the mind, but the one who hears it.

You are not the one who longs to die.
You are the space for the hurting self,
the despairing child inside.
The one who holds the longing.
The one who is still here.
Here, in spite of everything.
Hurting, exhausted, but still here.
The One who cannot die. Presence itself.

Feel your tired feet on the solid earth, friend.
Hear the sounds all around you.
Bless your aching heart, head, chest, belly.
(There is so much life even in the ache, isn't there?)

Your ancestors are with you now,
even though you cannot see them.
Your brothers and sisters all across the world,
supporting you now, willing you to go on,
even though you cannot feel them.
The Universe is holding you now. The Earth and
all the stars.
The mountains and the forests.
The oceans and the sky. All the gods in all the realms.

You don't need to take your life.
Just let your life be taken by all that you see.

Give yourself to this moment.
Fall to the ground.
Cry, scream. Be undignified!
There is no such thing as failure here.
You and life, as One. A divine madness.

You will tell the story one day of how love found you.
How you wanted to die, but found hope in a single breath.
In the birdsong. In the face of a stranger.
Someone curious about you. Someone who listened.

Today's fire has come to burn away the falseness.
And illuminate something yet unseen.

Have patience with the fire.
I can promise you:
You are destined for life.

PART FOUR

REASONS TO STAY ALIVE

C an we fall in love with the most ordinary moments of our days? Can we find our salvation in them?

A cup of tea. A walk to the post office to mail a letter. Sitting with a friend in silent contemplation.

Perhaps the Kingdom of Heaven is here, right here on Earth.

The most "enlightened" people I have ever met are actually the most human, too. The most "spiritually awake" ones often talk little of spirituality. Often they are not the teachers, spouting clever words about bliss, pure awareness, and the illusory nature of the separate self, making promises about "the end of suffering" that they cannot actually deliver. In my humble view, the most "awake" ones are the ones who have fallen in love with their ordinariness, who have cultivated a deep warm compassion for themselves, a profound self-kindness, a tenderness toward their own tired minds and aching bodies, and who radiate that delicious empathy into the world. One foot in awareness, yes, but the other foot dancing and playing in the gloriously weird mess of relative existence; courageous enough to receive both the ecstasy and agony of existence with humility and awe, courageous enough to admit that—ultimately—they do not know a damn thing.

Our humanness is not "less than" our divine nature; it is her expression and her fulfilment. Spiritual awakening has very little to do with transcending thoughts and feelings, denying our vulnerable humanity and attempting to escape into some state of pure awareness, some higher realm, some new dream.

Instead, let us bow to our sorrow, embrace it tenderly in our arms! Let us hold our doubts close as we walk the path of today. Let us see the sacredness in our fear, the joy in our confusion, the freedom in our anger. Let us prostrate ourselves before life in all her forms, not just the "pretty" ones.

"This world is too vast for us to know," said my eighty-four-year-old father, looking out over the English Channel, a few weeks before he died, unable to recall the past, his heart broken wide open to the present.

I know no spirituality that separates itself from the muddle, muck, and mess of relative existence. I know no spirituality that is unwilling to bow to the broken heart, saturate it with attention and breath; to flood the darkness with light, make friends with the radiant night.

So we are no longer numb. So we can meet each other in the fire.

It's true. It's really true. The world is too vast for us to know.

THE

LIGHT

Do not seek the light.
See it.

Do not look for beauty.
Be it.

Do not search for Self.
Know it.

Let the birdsong teach you.

Let the sunrise
break your heart open.

Let every breath
remind you of miracles.

HOW TO BREATHE WHEN YOU CAN HARDLY BREATHE

And then there are the days
where you can hardly breathe
because everything has turned
to beauty and iridescence.

Because you are a witness to this ordinary world.
The ordinary burning world
that lays itself out for you effortlessly,
in all its absurdity and sanctity,
in its compassion and its terror,
in its sorrow and its light.

All One. All Art.

And you are a Doorway today.
You are a Magic Theater
where the heart plays out
its paupers and its princesses
and pretends to fluff its lines.

Do you remember. Do you remember.
His first day at school?
How he slipped through your fingers then?
So eager to leave, and did he know?

The frosted spider webs clinging to the office bins
when you went out for a quick cigarette
and how they cracked you open without warning
and how they broke you open without warning
and how you couldn't tell a soul.
You had a secret with the spiders.

And then mother's courage.
Her snow-white hair tumbling out in your hands.
Her translucence in the last light.
Where you held her.
She had become see-through.

Some days. Some days.
You try to form words but none will come.
You try to write but the pen won't move.
You try to speak but the silence silences.
Some days are see-through too.

It matters not how much money you have.
Your status in this world.
The strength of your immune system.
The number of weeks you have left.

It matters how completely you inhabit this life.

How deeply you let the days penetrate.

And crack you.

And make you beg for more,

for less,

for more,

for less,

for more.

Don't be ashamed to break down today!

To weep.

To laugh.

To snort.

To dribble.

To not know.

To admit all your mistakes.

All your damn mistakes.

To begin again.

To be a puddle of nothing on the ground.

To be translucent and soft.

Awakening is not a hobby, friend.

It's a radical reframing of your entire existence.

It's the devastation of the dreamer.

And in the rubble, such intensity.

Such ferocity.

Such light.

In the devastation we can truly meet.

And knit with the spiders at dawn.
Giggle with the afternoon crows.

Play hide-and-seek with the grown-ups;
make them forget their melancholy,
if only for a moment.

Sing star-mantras with the wolves.
And live the days.

Somehow live through the days.

Where the beauty is just too relentless.
Where we haven't got the strength to stand.

Where we cannot breathe ourselves
and so Love breathes us instead,
and warms us from the inside,

and fills us with new hope
under an iridescent sky.

REJOICE,
NOTHING
LASTS

Rejoice, nothing lasts.
What is born must eventually return to source.

Every moment from now on, then,
is more precious, more worthy of your full attention,
your loving presence, your gratitude.

The dream of "more time"
can make us complacent,
send us to sleep
or make us gallop through our days in fear.

The shock of realizing
our absolute impermanence
and the impermanence of all we hold dear, and all we fear,
can wake us up.

Come on. Be sillier today.

Slow down today.
Let your heart pound and be penetrated today.
Make a fool of yourself today.

Give up the hope of finding happiness in the future,
and break open into the happiness
of this holy day,
this only day.

You really don't need
more time
to be present.

REASONS

TO

STAY

ALIVE

You don't need to kill yourself.
But you aren't "sick" or "damaged"
for contemplating it.

You are free. And your mind is free in your freedom.
Free to imagine futures. Free to contemplate death.
Free to fantasize.
To paint any image on the canvas of awareness,
however negative to the judgmental mind.

You are free to desire the end.
But you don't need to kill yourself.

You are tired, yes. You long for rest, of course.
You are sick of the world. I get it.
(Many are sick of the world,
but you have the courage to admit it.)

Your mind won't stop.
Minds aren't supposed to *stop*.

Your body aches.
Bodies are *built* to ache sometimes.

Minds and bodies just want love.
They ache for it sometimes.

Even though it may seem hopeless now,
you don't need to die.

Even though the life you long for
may seem light-years away.
Even though deep feelings of guilt, anxiety, fear,
and shame
may be surging in you now.
Even though you feel numb and disconnected
(and even if these words provide no home or hope).
Even though the day or night seems impossible to
get through,
you don't need to kill yourself.

For the self that wants to die is not the self that you are.
If you can kill it, it was an impostor.

You only want to be true
because you are true.
You only long for freedom
because you are already free.
Free to long for freedom.
Free to think about death.

It is a rough day, for sure, but not the end.

And the courage that brought you this far will carry you further.
And the life that is breathing you now will breathe you tomorrow.

You don't need to understand how to breathe.
You don't need to understand how to see, or hear, or taste.
You don't need to understand how to live.
You don't need to fix yourself.

You are not broken
even though you feel broken.

You don't need to kill yourself.
Just feel your feet on the ground.
Feel your belly rise and fall, now.
Hear the sounds all around you.
(What can you hear? Tell me, what can you hear?)
The sounds of the morning, the sounds of the
evening.
The thud and hum and buzz of life.

Moment by moment, friend.
Moment by moment.

We are all with you here, though you cannot see us.
We hold you close though you cannot feel us.
There is no disgrace in what you are going through.
We have all been through the burning.

You will write the book of your life one day.
You will inspire others with your courage.

Trust. And if you cannot trust now, then have faith.
And if you cannot have faith now, then at least
bow to your doubt.
And if you cannot bow today, then just let
everything go,
and lie naked under the still moon,
or let the warm ocean caress your feet,
or weep at your favorite song until your tear ducts
run dry,
and rest in the silence between tears.

Give up and give yourself to this soft world,
far softer than the mind's version of it.

In the end, we are all stripped down to the bone.

To presence.

We all lose everything, fall.

And we are invited to begin again.

Moment by moment.

Moment by moment.

That's all there is, in reality.

Rebuilding a life. An instant at a time.

That's all you ever have to face.

An instant at a time.

An old existence ends, and a new one begins.
A death, a rebirth.

You want to die,
you want to live.
You want to be here, anyway, to witness yourself
wondering.

To read these words.

To comprehend them, or not. To appreciate them or
hate them.

To keep going, even if the future seems bleak.

To live, even though there doesn't seem to be a reason.

To push through the meaninglessness and the pain
and know the glory:

"I wanted to die, yet I lived!"

Oh, you are a fucking warrior, my friend.

YOUR

LIFE'S

PURPOSE

Sometimes your purpose in life
is to have *no damn clue* what your purpose is.

And to wonder.
To explore.
To be silent.
To travel.
To not even believe in purpose.

That's the purpose, sometimes:
To doubt your purpose.

Sometimes the meaning of life
is to feel that life has no meaning.
To question.
To be disillusioned, stripped of illusions.
To lose faith.

That's the meaning, sometimes.
To wonder about meaning.

It feels so meaningful, to wonder, sometimes.
And full. And authentic. And close.

Nobody can take these things away from you:
Your questions. Your innocence.
Your wondering.
Your infinitely curious heart.

TRUST

THE

DARKNESS

NOW

If you are lost.

If nothing makes sense anymore.

If all your reference points have collapsed.

Breathe.

In, out.

In, out.

If the old life is crumbling now.

If the mind is foggy, tired, busy.

If the organism is exhausted and longs to rest.

Trust.

This is a rite of passage, not an error.

You are healing in your own original way.

You are not damaged.

You are not "screwed up."

You are not going mad.
You are not destined for the dung heap.

Contact the ground now.
Breathe.
In, out.
In, out.

Make room for the invitees:

The sorrow, doubt, fear, anger.

An ancient emptiness.

A longing.

This familiar taste of incompleteness.

They just want to pass through.

They just want to be felt.

They just want to be *known*.

You are a vessel, not a separate self.
You are a vast sky, not the passing weather.
Breathe.
In, out.
In, out.

Others may not understand.

Give them back their misunderstanding.

Celebrate the place where *you* are.

Celebrate your inability to celebrate sometimes.

Celebrate your total lack of interest in *celebrations*.

Contact the ground.

Breathe.
In, out.
In, out.

Breathe, friend.
In, out.
In, out.

LULLABY

FOR

THE

SEEKER

Welcome, again, weary one.
Rest.
Lay your head down.
You have traveled far, I see.

I still have no clever words for you.
No system to teach.
No image to maintain.

You'll find no philosophy here.
No answers to your many questions.

I offer only presence. Sanctuary.
A bed. A meal.
A small kindness to repay yours.

I am no better than you.
My guru is life.
My lineage is love.

I do not separate the enlightened from the unenlightened.
I teach nothing I do not live.
I quote not from books
but from the cracks in the heart.

I see your fragility
yet I see your immense power.

You are not broken.
You were never broken.
Don't let them tell you that you are broken.

We met long ago when dust settled to form worlds.
I think I saw your courage then.

Close your eyes.
I will keep watch tonight.

ABOUT THE AUTHOR

Jeff Foster is an author, poet, and spiritual teacher from the UK. He studied astrophysics at Cambridge University. In his early twenties, struggling with chronic shame and suicidal depression, he became addicted to the idea of "spiritual enlightenment" and began a near-obsessive spiritual quest for the ultimate truth of existence. The search came crashing down with the discovery of nonduality and the simple joy of Presence. For over a decade Jeff has been offering meetings and retreats around the world, inviting people into a place of radical self-acceptance and deep rest. He now also offers online courses. His website is lifewithoutacentre.com.

ABOUT SOUNDS TRUE

Sounds True is a multimedia publisher whose mission is to inspire and support personal transformation and spiritual awakening. Founded in 1985 and located in Boulder, Colorado, we work with many of the leading spiritual teachers, thinkers, healers, and visionary artists of our time. We strive with every title to preserve the essential "living wisdom" of the author or artist. It is our goal to create products that not only provide information to a reader or listener but also embody the quality of a wisdom transmission.

For those seeking genuine transformation, Sounds True is your trusted partner. At SoundsTrue.com you will find a wealth of free resources to support your journey, including exclusive weekly audio interviews, free downloads, interactive learning tools, and other special savings on all our titles.

To learn more, please visit SoundsTrue.com/freegifts or call us toll-free at 800.333.9185.